SAINT PATRICK

A Life From Beginning to End

Copyright © 2018 by Hourly History.

All rights reserved.

Table of Contents

Introduction

Known as the patron saint of Ireland, Saint Patrick was a missionary who is best known for converting Ireland to Christianity in the fifth century CE. He is the stuff of legend and of truth, beloved by many, and thus it can be difficult to discern which stories are factual and which are not. Many of them are borne of the joy and new way of life brought to the nation by Patrick.

One may be surprised to learn that Saint Patrick was not actually an Irishman. His name was not Patrick either—this was a name chosen by him after joining the clergy and becoming a priest. Saint Patrick is celebrated by Catholics and idolized by millions due to his resilience, kindness, and numerous good works that he perpetuated. He was an unlikely candidate for such a task, having little to no religious education while growing up. His visions would have him seek a path even he felt was unlikely. It was certainly no easy task to bring Christianity to an entire nation, but by gathering a band of loyal followers, walking miles and miles, preaching, and teaching the ways of Christ, millions of Irish citizens found themselves practicing Christianity.

Scholars are unsure of when Patrick took his last breath. He is presumed to have died on March 17, 493 CE, in Saul, County Down. It is for this reason modern society celebrates Saint Patrick's Day every year on March 17. Many traditions of Saint Patrick's Day derive from the practices of the saint. For example, the tradition of Pota

Phadraig (or Patrick's Pot) is the name given to the amount of whiskey to be drank on Saint Patrick's Day. It is customary to float a shamrock upon the whiskey before drinking it. Whether Christian or not, the story of Saint Patrick is an intriguing and remarkable one.

Chapter One

From Slave to Bishop

"And He watched over me before I knew Him and before I learned sense or even distinguished between good and evil."

—Saint Patrick

Saint Patrick's birthplace is not exactly known. Religious scholars believe he was born around the year 375 CE in Scotland, but other accounts indicate that the location could have been Cumberland, England, or even in Northern Wales.

Patrick referred to himself as being Roman and Briton. He was born to Calpurnius and Conchessa, Roman parents living in Britain. Calpurnius was a deacon and came from a family of high social status. Conchessa meanwhile was a relative of the patron saint of Tours, Saint Martin. Beyond that, Patrick's grandfather, Pontius, was a clergyman. Patrick was born under the name Maewyn Succat and only changed his name after becoming a priest. Oddly enough, his family did not place emphasis on religion or education—neither was particularly impressed upon him while growing up. Patrick described his embarrassment about it in his *Confessio*, stating that he feared to reveal his lack of education.

When Patrick was 16 years old, he was taken captive by Irish pirates. He and several of his father's slaves and vassals were brought to Ireland, where they were sold into slavery. He ended up in the city of Dalriada; his job there was to tend sheep. During his time as a shepherd, Patrick often suffered from cold and hunger.

Patrick answered to a pagan master whose name was Milchu. Milchu was a high priest in the religion of druidism, which reigned supreme in Ireland during this period. Even though Patrick had been a non-believer up to this point in his life, he saw his enslavement as a test of faith from God. He thus devoted himself to Christianity and prayed constantly. His prayers would not go unanswered.

One night Patrick received what he perceived as an important message. In a dream, he saw all the children of Ireland still inside their mothers' wombs reaching their small hands out to him. He interpreted the vision to be a call to do mission work in pagan Ireland. His faith renewed, Patrick was grateful for the Lord having taken mercy on his youthful and ignorant soul and was elated with the opportunity to have his sins forgiven and become a devoted Christian. This opportunity, coupled with the message that he had received, propelled him onward.

Patrick eventually escaped after six harrowing years in captivity. The escape happened around 408 CE, inspired by another dream in which a voice told him he was going to find his way home to Britain and that "Your ship awaits you." Patrick felt he had to make the dream come true, and so he fled from his master and headed south, traveling over 200 miles. When he reached the town of Wexford, he approached some sailors and convinced them to allow him to board their ship. The journey from Ireland began.

The crew sailed for three days before they reached the coast where they abandoned their vessel. They wandered in the wilderness for 28 days and covered hundreds of miles of terrain in the process of doing so. The starving crew had no supplies left and became faint from lack of food. Advising his shipmates to put their faith in God, Patrick prayed for sustenance and, before long, encountered a herd of wild boar. This event greatly contributed to his reputation and esteem within the group.

Patrick eventually found his way home in his early twenties, around the age of 22. He was reunited with his family and would continue his study of Christianity. He is presumed to have studied mainly in France, spending years in a town called Auxerre. Although his studies were carried out here, he is also thought to have visited Tours and the Abbey of Marmoutier. He is also presumed to have received his tonsure (shaving of the hair from the scalp as an act of humility) at Lérins Abbey, which is located on an island off the French coast.

Patrick performed most of his studies under the guidance of a missionary named Saint Germanus, who was a bishop of the Western Church. Saint Germanus was a fine teacher for Patrick; he had abandoned his career as a high-ranking official of the government to devote his life to the church. Saint Germanus cared about promoting his beliefs and his church and strived to protect his flock during dangerous times. For example, he would later go on to fight to combat Pelagianism in 429 CE and confront a barbarian king named Goar around 440 CE. His drive and devotion matched that of Patrick's, and Patrick learned much from this holy man. His studies paid off, and he was ordained as a deacon by Saint Germanus in approximately 418 CE.

No matter how time passed, Patrick never lost sight of his ultimate goal to share his newfound beliefs with the Irish. Just a few years after he left Ireland, a vision containing a man named Victoricus appeared to him. Victoricus brought letters to Patrick, and one of these letters was called "The Voice of the Irish." While reading the letter, Patrick imagined he could hear the voices of the people in the forest of Foclut, located by the Western Sea. Their message was clear: they wanted Patrick to come and walk among them. Some religious scholars argue that Victoricus of Patrick's vision may be Saint Victricius, a bishop of Rouen and a missionary who was known to have visited Britain approximately 396 CE.

In 432 CE, Patrick became a bishop at the age of 43 and was ordered by Pope Celestine I to Ireland to share the gospel to all the non-believers, as well as extend support to the Christians already residing there.

Chapter Two

Patrick Returns as a Missionary

"I most certainly believe that it is the gift of God that I am what I am. And so, I dwell amongst barbarians, a proselyte and an exile, for the love of God."

—Saint Patrick

Upon arriving in Ireland, Patrick decided to join other early missionaries, all intent on converting the Irish pagans to Christianity. He first landed in Wicklow, which sits at the mouth of the river called Inver-dea (today known as the Vartry). Wicklow is a place of rich history, the county being the last of the traditional counties of Ireland to be shired in 1606. Wicklow features an early monastic site situated in Glendalough, which survives to this day. Some scholars also suggest that Patrick made his escape from slavery from the port in Wicklow and not Wexford, which is located around 50 miles south of Wicklow.

Not everyone in Ireland welcomed Patrick's arrival and mission. Hostile locals drove him out, forcing him to travel north in search of more willing subjects. Several warlords and kings felt threatened by the work of Patrick.

Patrick often paid penance (or bribes) so that he could have a safe passage through the areas in which these kings and warlords reigned. He paid the bribes and used the rulers to access their lands, as they had used Patrick to curry favor and gain wealth with Christians. Although the paying of such sums is often viewed in a negative light, Patrick did not regret paying bribes. He even indicated he would be willing to pay more if it meant that he could spread his message.

Patrick took a respite at the islands off the Skerries coastline, and even today, one of the of those islands is called Inis-Patrick or Saint Patrick's Island. Patrick eventually made his way to Saul, where he found his first sanctuary. Saul is a significant place, known as the "Cradle of Christianity" in the country of Ireland. Here, Patrick and his followers encountered a local chief named Dichu, whom Patrick quickly converted to Christianity. It was this same convert who offered the missionaries a barn for shelter. Saul is said to be the earliest place of Christian worship in Ireland.

Followers continued to convert and join Patrick. One notable follower was Benin (sometimes known as Beningus). He was the son of the chieftain Secsnen and eagerly joined Patrick's group. Benin was baptized into the Christian faith by Patrick and eventually became his favorite disciple. Benin followed Patrick in all of his travels and was of great help in various missionary work. He was especially integral in the development of choral services, which was very appropriate as his family was likely part of the bardic order. His musical talents were so renowned, he became known as "Patrick's psalm-singer." Benin was trained from his youth by Patrick and well-versed in the languages of his land. He thus became the prime candidate to become secretary to the Commission of Nine, which was tasked with compiling early Irish laws. Benin is also said to have been a contributor to various religious texts, including works like the Psalter of Cashel and the Book of Rights.

Patrick soon learned from Dichu about a special feast to be celebrated at Tara. It was at this gathering that Patrick knew he could take a stand against Druidism, which was the religion commonly practiced in Ireland at the time. Patrick felt he could bring redemption and would serve as God's herald to share these glad tidings.

Chapter Three

The Feast at Tara

"We entreat thee, holy youth, to come and walk still among us."

—Saint Patrick

The Hill of Tara is located near the Boyne River and is the site of the feast that took place in approximately 433 CE. It was hosted by Laoghaire, the supreme monarch of Ireland at that time. A decree was sent throughout the kingdom that the day before the feast, all fires were to be put out to allow the great festival fire at Tara to burn alone. Chieftains and Brehons as well as druids came forth, each ready to muster their strength and resist the work of Patrick. Their goal was to hold onto their Celtic ways of life, as—the legend goes—their oracles had given them a premonition that a messenger of Christ had come forth to Erin.

Patrick made his way to the Hill of Slane, which was opposite Tara, on the night before Easter. On that hill, Patrick kindled the Paschal fire, to which the druids immediately voiced their concerns. They decreed that the fire would burn forever in defiance of the royal edict unless it could be extinguished that very same night. Attempts were made to put out the blessed fire, and death was to be bestowed upon whoever disobeyed the royal command. The fire kept on burning brightly, however, and Patrick was spared from harm.

The following day was Easter, and Patrick, followed by his band of missionaries and his loyal follower Benin, walked along holding a copy of the Gospels. Patrick was dressed in full episcopal garb, complete with mitre and crozier. Armed with faith, the group made their way to Tara, walking in processional order.

According to the legend, the druids and magicians could not slow down Patrick and his band of loyal followers. They kept murmuring incantations, put forth every bit of their strength, and tried their hardest, but the power of prayer and faith reigned supreme. Patrick and the rest of his followers emerged triumphant. The druids, on the other hand, had unleashed so many incantations that the sky turned dark and spread over the hill in a dark cloud. Patrick challenged the druids to remove the cloud, but their efforts were in vain. Patrick responded by praying, at which the sun emerged from behind the clouds, set down some beautiful rays, and lit up the land with its light. One druid by the name of Lochru attempted to counterattack, but upon prayer from Patrick, he fell down, his head striking a boulder so hard that he died.

This marks the end of paganism in the presence of all its chieftains, assembled there at Tara. A young page, Erc, rose to show Patrick reverence. A chief and bard named Dubhatch also showed honor to Patrick and ended up becoming a disciple of the church. And it was on this occasion that one of Saint Patrick's symbols, the shamrock, came to be known. It is here that the legend states Patrick picked a shamrock from a small patch of grass and showed the chieftains how the tiny plant represented the Holy Trinity: the Father, the Son, and the Holy Ghost.

Thus, completed the feast at Tara that Easter Sunday. Even though he remained a pagan, Laoghaire was so impressed by Patrick's courage and faith that he granted him the right to preach his faith all through the land and acknowledged that the sacred fire started by him would never go out or be extinguished. One might consider reading the prayer known as "St. Patrick's Breast Plate," which is presumed to have been written by Patrick in preparation for victory over the pagan followers.

Patrick stayed at Tara and Slane the following week. He preached the lessons of divine truth to all those around him. Patrick also proceeded with the baptism of Laoghaire's brother, Conall, on April 5, 433. Meanwhile, other followers, including Benin, had already privately gathered in the church for baptism. Baptisms were going public effective April 5. This is the day viewed by many as they day Ireland began getting baptized.

It is also around this time the first Christian chieftain made the fateful gift of a church to Patrick. Some of the chieftains who had come to Tara were from Foclut, and they wanted to be among the first to receive the good tidings and redemption from Patrick.

These events are thought to be the stuff of legend for some but for others provide an account of the adversity Patrick overcame in his quest to preach his newfound faith to the people of Ireland. Despite having proven his faith and the power of redemption, he still would face adversity among rulers while attempting to make his way through the land to deliver his message. It is here we come to learn that Patrick would sometimes have to pay his way in order to guarantee himself safe passage.

From here, Patrick made his way around the country, ridding areas like Magh Slécht of idol-worship. According to legend, Magh Slécht was home to a huge stone pillar covered in gold and silver with a dozen or so minor statues surrounding the pillar. The site was used for human sacrifice rituals and worship of the Sun-God, Crom Cruach. Patrick set to work smiting the chief idol. It crumbled into a pile of dust, and the other ones simply fell to the ground in defeat.

Some areas did not require such a show of force and were ready to receive Patrick's message. For example, upon reaching Killala, the entire population was assembled and ready to learn. It was there that Killala's king and his six sons, plus 12,000 of the territory's people, listened raptly and adopted their newfound faith. Over the next seven years, Patrick would visit each and every district in Connaught, where he organized parishes, formed dioceses, and taught chieftains and their constituents the ways of the faith.

Perhaps the most unusual and remarkable encounter for the Patrick and his followers happened when Ethne and Fedelm, daughters of King Laoghaire, approached their camp. The women were getting ready to bathe as they approached but soon began to ask if the missionaries were friends or foe. Patrick responded by telling them about the one true God, whom they would be better off adoring. The two young women, specifically Ethne, launched into a series of questions in which she asked about God and who he was. And it was after a series of questions the two young women agreed to learn how they could serve God.

Patrick asked if they believed in the resurrection on Judgement Day, if they believed in penance after sin, and if they believed in the unity of the church. After responding yes, the women were baptized and clothed in white; they also received the sacrifice, the Eucharist of God.

Slowly but surely, Patrick was bringing a new lifestyle and belief system to a country permeated by pagan beliefs. In his view, his work did much to honor Christ and promote values of peace and goodwill. Patrick knew he was in danger doing this. He expected to be murdered, betrayed, or even brought back to slavery if someone was given the opportunity. But his belief in the afterlife and eternal salvation kept him pressing onward; Patrick fully believed that Heaven awaited him so long as he believed in Christ as his lord and savior.

Chapter Four

Ireland's First Martyr

*"Christ beside me, Christ before me, Christ behind me,
Christ within me, Christ beneath me, Christ above me."*

—Saint Patrick

Patrick began the task of converting Ulster in 440 CE. Ulster is a province located in the north of the nation of Ireland. It contains nine counties, thereby illustrating the mountainous task that Patrick had ahead of him. Patrick had help from annals, who laid forth a great spread of the faith throughout the Ulster province. Patrick was certainly eager to begin converting the Irish to Christianity. He was serving in a region of Ireland where few outsiders had traveled. As he roamed, he preached his message to pagans and gave instruction to Christian believers, training others to aid in the teachings of Christianity and ordaining native clergy.

It is presumed that Patrick settled in Armagh, a city that would forever be affected by Patrick's legacy. Upon his first visit, he called the city "sweet hill." Even today, Armagh is considered to be the religious capital of Ireland, and there are not one but two breathtaking cathedrals that bear Patrick's name.

In 444 CE, a church site was granted for Armagh by the chieftain Daire, who presided over that district. Daire appointed land at the foot of a hill, but Patrick was not content with the placement of the church. Patrick had a special design within his heart and mind for that particular district, and after speaking with Daire, he was granted permission to choose any site he wanted within the chieftain's territory. It was then that Patrick chose the breathtaking Hill of Armagh on which to construct his first large church made of stone.

The story goes that when Patrick and his band of missionaries were preparing to begin construction of the church, they came upon two animals. A doe and her fawn stood in the wild. The missionaries were wont to kill them for their meat, but Patrick immediately told them not to do so. Instead, Patrick put the fawn upon his shoulders and began walking. The doe followed him closely. Patrick made his way to a neighboring hill. It was there that he laid down the fawn. He made a special announcement: it was at this very hill that in future times, supreme glory would be given to God. And as Patrick proclaimed, a cathedral was dedicated upon that hill, presided over by the Holy See and gathered around by hundreds of holy men including priests and bishops. It is said that Ireland offered the glorious cathedral to God as evidence of their faith and endless love for him.

It is presumed that after Ulster, Patrick made his way to Meath. This county is situated in the mid-east region of Ireland and named after its kingdom of the same name. Patrick came to this region as a means of consolidating the many community groups that made up the area. He continued onward through Leinster, accompanied still by his band of missionaries.

He was especially assisted by two companions of high esteem to Patrick, Saint Auxilius and Saint Iserninus. The two were assigned to bring the good word to the valley of the Liffey, situated near the river that runs through the city of Dublin. Saint Iserninus is known for having founded a church at Killossy, and Saint Auxilius is known for being the very first bishop of Kilcullen. The two forged onward, while Patrick's primary concern was to convince and educate the ruling chieftains of the word of God.

The first conversion of this region took place at Naas, the site of the royal residence. The process took off well as Patrick baptized two royal sons of the king of Leinster. Patrick even founded a church there, and memorials honoring the saint and his work remain within the city. At Sletty, a parish located near the town of Carlow in northwest Ireland, Saint Fiacc made his debut as a bishop, thereby transforming that parish into the center of religious education for all of Leinster.

After doing these good works, Patrick made his way into Gowran and then into the kingdom of Ossory, where he built another church. This church's construction took place under the blessing of Saint Martin. Saint Martin enriched the church with relics he had procured from Rome. The church, known as Domhnach Mór, was located in the city of Kilkenny; the site is today home to St. Patrick's Graveyard.

Patrick's missionaries were fiercely loyal to him, a testament to his character. In one instance, Patrick's chariot driver, Odran, overheard that a chieftain of the Leinster region worshipped Crom Cruach, the pagan Sun-God. The chieftain, apparently angered by Patrick's destruction of the ritual site Magh Slécht, was involved in a plot to murder Patrick. Plans were being made to kill Patrick while he rode in the chariot. The next time Odran and Patrick set out to continue their journey, Odran asked Patrick to take the reins for him so that he may rest and recover. By doing this, the lance intended for Patrick's heart was instead pierced into Odran's heart. This simple changing of places was enough to save the beloved saint and grant Odran the martyr's crown; he became the first Christian martyr in Ireland. Odran's murderer was eventually convicted and executed for his crime.

After this incident, Patrick made his way to the region of Munster, located in the south of Ireland. Here, his efforts were mainly devoted to convincing the chieftains about their erroneous beliefs and replacing them with the ones that follow Christian teachings. He knew that by converting the local chieftains, the citizens of these areas soon would follow.

In the area of the Rock of Cashel, also known as Cashel of the Kings or St. Patrick's Rock, Patrick was received with great joy and high regard. According to local mythology, the Rock of Cashel was created when Patrick banished Satan from a cave, which caused the Rock to land in Cashel. It's said that Patrick converted the king of Munster at this site.

Patrick was also engaged in the baptism of the royal prince Aengus, son of the king of Munster. It was during this baptism that Patrick while leaning on his crosier accidentally pierced the foot of the young prince. Aengus simply bore the pain, not flinching in the slightest. It was at the close of the ceremony that Patrick noticed blood flowing from the prince's foot. Patrick asked the young man why he had remained quiet throughout the ceremony despite the injury. Aengus replied with the voice of a hero and stated that he thought it part of the ceremony, nothing more than a simple penalty for the blessings that Christ bestowed upon the people. Patrick was moved by the prince's heroism and took the chieftain's shield. He inscribed the shield with the point of the crozier and made a promise that the shield would be a signal of endless spiritual and temporal victories.

Chapter Five

Apostle Life

"I have had the good fortune through my God that I should never abandon his people whom I have acquired in the extremities of the earth."

—Saint Patrick

Patrick also spent plenty of time in the County of Limerick. The word had spread about Patrick and the miracles and sanctity he brought with him. Thus, the denizens of Thomond and northern Munster yearned to receive his teachings. They crossed the River Shannon in small, weak coracle boats, eager to hear the good word. Patrick was giving the people his blessing upon the summit of the Finnime hill when he looked out on the plains in front of him. It was at this moment he prophesied the arrival of Saint Senan. He proclaimed that to the green island of the west, at the mouth of the sea, a light sent from God would come to the people. He also indicated that Senan would be the head of religious counsel to all people of this area. And it was so—the holy wells of Senan remain, as well as the rock he used for his bed, and also the altar on which the daily Holy Sacrifice was offered.

Patrick spent seven years preaching in the Munster province. Whether he was on the banks of the Suir, the Blackwater, or the Lee, he was greeted with a warm and hearty welcome. It is said that after Patrick founded churches and places of worship in Munster, had ordained men of various spiritual grades, healed the sick, and raised the dead, he wished the people a warm farewell and also bestowed his blessing upon the people. The blessing was given from the hills of Tipperary, a beautiful mountainous region in Munster. Patrick blessed the people with a prayer that called forth a bountiful land filled with plenty of fruits for all the citizens. The prayer also called forth a blessing on each person that they would never want for help with money, that treasure would always be available. Patrick also called for a blessing upon the mountains, glens, and ridges of Munster. The prayer closed with a request for blessings in all areas of the Munster province—a blessing as prominent as the sand in every hearth, slope, plain, mountain, and hill.

Patrick continued his journey as an apostle, watching over the churches he had founded all over the nation of Ireland. He would visit with his believers, comforting them in times of difficulty. He made sure their faith in the Christian teaching was of the utmost strength and that their virtue held strong, too. He also appointed pastors as a means of providing guidance and counsel to his flock. Patrick is said to have consecrated no less than 350 bishops. He is also credited with appointing Saint Loman to Trim, which matched Armagh in its abundance of piousness. Even more remarkable is the appointing of

Saint Guasach, who was the son of Patrick's former master Milchu. Saint Guasach became the bishop of Granard. Meanwhile the two daughters of Milchu founded a convent for themselves and other pious virgins. Saint Mel, Patrick's nephew, took charge of Ardagh, while Saint MacCarthem, loved dearly by Patrick, was made to be the bishop of Clogher.

Despite the hard work that Patrick had been doing, there were still chieftains and others in need of conversion. It was at this time he met with Ernasc, a chieftain in the Costello district in County Mayo. Patrick found Ernasc and his son Loarn sitting underneath a tree. Patrick and his missionaries sat down with the two men, educating them for an entire week of the gospel. Father and son received the information with a very attentive ear and mindset. Loarn especially was instructed in the ways of piety and learning. A church was built on their land, and Loarn was appointed as its charge in due time.

It is said that Patrick was truly the embodiment of all the traits of saints before him. If Patrick was not spreading the good word, he was almost always enveloped in prayer. He armed himself daily with the sign of the cross and never broke his holy exercises. Patrick chose to live simply, devoting everything he had to the gospel of Christ. He chose to wear a rough hair-shirt. The hair-shirt was not just a humble peasant garment; rather, it was worn around the loins or as a shirt in a show of mortification as well as penance. A similar garment was worn by John the Baptist and would help resist temptations of the flesh. The garment was worn by holy and common citizens alike, as it was clothing that provided an antidote against luxury and comfort. Aside from wearing simple and relatively uncomfortable clothing, Patrick also chose to take his rests upon a hard rock. Often times, converts of high rank would come to pay their respects to Patrick, laying ornaments of value and preciousness at his feet. But Patrick would not have any of these earthly treasures; he had come to Ireland for the sole purpose of promoting the message and gift of the Catholic faith, not for material possessions or wealth.

His good works, humble nature, and desire to preach the message of Jesus Christ was a priority he placed above all others.

Chapter Six

Letter to the Soldiers of Coroticus

"Now you, Coroticus—and your gangsters, rebels all against Christ, now where do you see yourselves? You gave away girls like prizes: not yet women, but baptized. All for some petty temporal gain that will pass in the very next instant."

—Saint Patrick

Patrick is credited for many good works that he performed during his time in Ireland. Perhaps the most famous legend surrounding Saint Patrick is the way in which he drove all snakes from Ireland, causing the island to be free from serpents to this day. The story goes that Patrick chased the snakes into the sea because they attacked him while he was fasting on top of a hill. There is however no evidence to suggest that snakes have been part of Ireland's fauna since the last ice age.

Other stories seem more credible. During Patrick's time as a missionary in fifth-century Ireland, he was not only a hero to his appointed clergymen, but to women as well. At this time, women were seen as property, a commodity to be bought or sold. It was not uncommon for a family to sell a daughter or arrange a marriage that would benefit them politically or monetarily. Patrick upset this order of operations by informing women that they did not have to choose this path—they had a choice in Jesus Christ. As these women made the conversion to Christianity, some opted to become servants for Christ. This was not without strong opposition from their families. Patrick remained firm and informed the women they were certainly doing right by Christ by choosing to remain chaste, or virgins for Christ. The sense of control women felt over their own destinies was empowering, but many men were angered as they felt their possessions were being taken away.

Patrick is also credited with having brought a sense of importance regarding learning and literacy to Ireland. During this period, the Roman Empire was facing collapse, and many politicians and philosophers believed it was the end of civilized society as the world knew it. Christians in other parts of the world did not feel that the Irish could be saved, or that they were even worthy of such salvation. Patrick changed this mindset with his bringing of the Christian faith to Ireland. In doing so, he promoted the importance of studying Scriptures and reading texts that had been written by faithful servants of the church.

Not everyone was pleased with the work Patrick was doing in Ireland however. Perhaps the most famous example of this is that of King Coroticus. King Coroticus essentially sought to chastise Patrick and his flock by taking them as slaves. Patrick, enraged because his flock was being sold into bondage as he had been so many years ago, confronted the king. He was met with nothing more than ridicule, and as a result, wrote the *Epistola*, excommunicating all of them from the faith.

Patrick writes in his *Epistola*, which was a letter to the soldiers of King Coroticus, that he grieves for the loss of his Christian brothers and sisters, as well as the loss of King Coroticus and his men from the Christian faith. Patrick denounces the king and his men, illustrating their barbaric and sinister ways by stating that any among the holy people would be horrified to interact with these people. He goes on to say that their homes are filled with items taken from dead Christians.

Patrick indicates that the church mourned for the loss of the sons and daughters who were taken and dropped far away to distant lands where sin runs rampant. He writes that the church weeps at the thought of fellow Christians being sold off and reduced to slaves. Patrick also makes note of his inability to provide aid or assistance to the men and women of Christ, noting that the evil of all evil has prevailed over the flock. He writes from a place of sadness, knowing that King Coroticus and his men had received the same baptism as the now-slaves. He also indicates that the practice goes against the very teachings of the Bible—the abandoning of neighbors and failing to render aid to a countryman in need is certainly a misstep in the Christian belief system.

Patrick writes that he grieves heavily for the loss of his flock. Yet he discovers the silver lining—he knows that his teachings have not been in vain after all. Patrick takes comfort in knowing that no matter what happens to the men and women of the faith, they will always find eternal salvation and life in Christ. In his words, the wicked will be as ashes under the feet of the once-captured slaves. He writes that they will live among the likes of apostles, prophets, and even martyrs as they take possession of a kingdom eternal. Meanwhile, Patrick also writes that wrongdoers will be left in an eternal fire-pit.

After expressing his grief regarding the captured flock, Patrick moves onto a discussion of the soldiers of Coroticus. Patrick indicates that these sinners, who perform such acts as treating baptized women as prizes or enslaving innocent Christians, will not find salvation. He mourns their evil ways, noting it is for an earthly, temporary kingdom that will not last forever. He indicates that only the just—not people like these soldiers carrying out heinous acts—will live in eternity with Christ.

Patrick closes his message by indicating that the letter should be delivered by a courageous servant of Christ and that it should be read to all, especially King Coroticus. Patrick believed that by doing so, the message might inspire the king and his men to realize that what they were doing was wrong and in need of correction. Patrick stated that even though the evil act had already taken place, there was still time for King Coroticus and his men to repent for what they had done. Patrick urged them to release their prisoners, such as the women they had taken as property and their Christian slaves. In this manner, Patrick said, they could live for God and still earn eternal salvation in the kingdom of Christ.

Chapter Seven

Confessio: A Brief Look

"I am Patrick, a sinner, most uncultivated and least of all the faithful and despised in the eyes of many."

—Saint Patrick

Saint Patrick's *Epistola* seems to have been written before his *Confessio*, which scholars believe was penned during the latter part of his life. In the *Confessio*, Patrick looks back on his life and gives an account of his mission in Ireland.

Although the *Confessio* is not very detailed, Patrick does mention a time when he was put on trial by his fellow Christians. The charges are not explicitly stated, but they are indicative of Patrick's peers believing he desired to rise through the ranks of religious hierarchy for personal gain. Some historians have suggested that the trial was instigated after Patrick sent his *Epistola* to King Coroticus and excommunicated him and his soldiers from the church. This act, they say, turned fellow Christians against Patrick and caused them to accuse him of accepting money and gifts in exchange for holy services like baptisms or the ordainment of priests. Patrick himself denies having accepted any gifts from wealthy converts, often returning gifts in favor of converting others for the right reasons of salvation and eternal life.

Perhaps the most interesting thing about the *Confessio* is that we do not see many of the popular images associated with Saint Patrick; for example, there are no shamrock references or mention of his famous Paschal fire. It does, however, provide a fascinating look at the life of Saint Patrick and how he perceived himself; the opening line has Patrick billing himself as a simple country person and a sinner at that.

The *Confessio* also describes Patrick's faith and his belief in God. He writes about recognizing his own failings as a child of God and using this opportunity to open his heart to God. The *Confessio* goes on to describe Patrick's testimony of faith, brought upon by a formal decree that concerns the Holy Trinity. Patrick gives acknowledgment to one God in a trinity of his sacred name. By examining these confessions, it appears that Patrick is attempting to lay out the orthodoxy of his religious beliefs.

Patrick then goes on to discuss the success of his mission, giving all glory to God. He indicates that without the grace of God, the mission could not have been successful. Patrick indicates that it is God who has strengthened him in all things he has attempted and granted him an understanding of the teachings of Jesus Christ. He argues that the faith given to him by God passed the test of his people, his followers. He goes on to say that his faith has left him with a debt to God. Patrick indicates he is grateful for the grace given to him so that many could be born again and brought to a full and meaningful life. He shows gratitude to the clergyman that are ordained or in the process of being ordained so that others can come and learn the good news of Christ and his teachings.

Perhaps the trial and criticism brought to him by others drove Patrick to write this testimony, confession, and declaration of his true faith in God. Patrick indicates that he was subject to criticism from people around him, including some he referred to as his superiors. Patrick says that during his work as a bishop, he was put to the test by some of the people he thought of as his betters. Testing his hard work as a bishop, these superiors brought forth a charge against Patrick about something that had occurred in his past. A close friend, whom Patrick had spoken to about the incident, betrayed the confidence of the saint, which was how the secret got out.

Thirty years previously, Patrick had confessed to something before he was even a deacon. Feeling rather down and poorly about himself regarding the matter, he confessed to a friend about the matter. He was only fifteen years old at the time and had not yet been versed in the ways of God, nor did he believe in God. Patrick indicates he was not able to overcome his weakness at such a young and uneducated age. The pain Patrick felt because of his friend's transgression is apparent in the *Confessio*, where he recounts the mixed messages given to him by his supposed friend. In one instance the friend had defended him while he was absent; another time the friend had disgraced him publicly for the incident he had already disclosed and been forgiven for.

Ultimately, Patrick wrote the *Confessio* as a means of showing his true love and devotion to God. He was conscious of his own flaws as illustrated in the *Confessio*, and he also made sure to attribute all success and triumphs in educating and converting Ireland to God. Patrick writes that he was nothing more than a stone in the mud until God came and pulled him out. He felt nothing but gratitude toward God for doing this and felt the need to repay such a kind deed by spreading the gospel for others to hear.

Patrick states that he will faithfully and without any fear spread the name of God so that even after he has died, he can leave something of value behind to his flock and fellow Irishmen. Patrick acknowledges he is not worthy of the beautiful gift God gives all, but accepts it fully, and again credits God for being the source of his strength.

In a further testament of Patrick's desire to spread the word of Christianity, he recounts his growth as an ignorant young man in captivity all the way to his current state. For example, he discusses the fervent nature of his prayers while a slave for Milchu. Thanks to his prayers and belief, he was able to overcome a temptation from Satan, break free from the chains that bound him in slavery, and receive a call from God to deliver the message to the Irish. The delivery of the message was no series of constant victories. Rather, it was the complete opposite. The saint was often the subject of trials by the hands of druids and other non-believers. In one part of the

Confessio, Patrick notes that his companions and himself were taken captive and carried off no less than a dozen times. On one of these occasions, Patrick was bound in chains and decreed to die. Despite all this, the saint continued onward in a show of his faith and desire to tell the nation about the joy of Christ.

Patrick closes the *Confessio* by imploring those who say they believe in God to believe him. He prays for all those who believe in and have respect for God. Patrick ends the text by stating that this was his confession before he dies.

Chapter Eight

Patrick on the Mount

"The Lord opened the understanding of my unbelieving heart, so that I should recall my sins."

—Saint Patrick

As Patrick's life continued onward, he proceeded to visit and watch over all the holy houses of worship that he had founded in provinces across the nation of Ireland. He would come to the faithful during their most difficult hours, offering them comfort and helping them grow in their beliefs. He strengthened them in the art of virtue and appointed various pastors to serve the people and continue his work.

Patrick would occasionally break from his spiritual tasks and duties of being an apostle to devote himself and his time to penance and prayer. He had a few places he would turn to for solitude, one of which was an island in the lake of Lough Derg. Also known as St. Patrick's Purgatory, Station Island is where Patrick would often retreat to pray and repent. There was also a place of worship honoring Patrick's miracles in the west of Ireland that he would sometimes visit; the tall, rugged mountains that make up the region keep out the waves of the ocean and provide a quiet place for reflection and learning.

One mountain, in particular, remains strongly connected to Saint Patrick. Known as Eagle Mountain by the pagans during their reign, the mountain eventually became known as Croagh Patrick, or St. Patrick's Mountain. It sits at an elevation of about 2,500 feet, facing Clew Bay and casting a shadow over neighboring cities of Aghagower and Westport. It is now honored as the Holy Hill or Ireland's own Mount Sinai. It's said that Patrick listened to the words of his special guardian angel and made this mountain his sacred, hallowed place of retreat. It was on this mountain that Patrick spent 40 days in a state of prayer. He also fasted and performed other exercises as a means of penance. He took shelter only in a cave to save himself from the harsh elements such as rain, wind, snow, and hail. This rather spartan recess was his only form of housing and is preserved and honored to this day.

Patrick's solitude and prayer upon the mountain was not an easy task in and of itself, and the legend goes that it was not made any simpler with the advent of demons and other creatures that sought to destroy and disturb the saint. Evil spirits and demons that made Ireland their battleground gathered all their strength and might and attempted to push Patrick away from his holy work. The demons took the form of several flocks of birds of prey. The ranks of these birds were dense, and they surrounded the mountain like a thick storm cloud. They filled the air so tightly Patrick could not see land or ocean, or sky, for that matter. Patrick then called upon God to disperse the demons, but at first nothing happened.

It seemed for the saint that his prayers were not being heard, that his efforts were in vain. Patrick then took it upon himself to ring his bell, and the pleasant, sweet sound carried throughout the valleys and hills all across Ireland. The Bell of Saint Patrick was a symbol of Patrick's preaching of the divine truth. Bells were used as a means of calling parishioners to prayer and were bestowed upon leaders of the new Christian communities that Patrick had founded. They were used to bring believers together for religious gatherings and during holy ceremonies as well. The story goes that Patrick rang his bell, and the beautiful sound resonated across Ireland, sending peace and joy all over the nation. The demons began to disperse and scatter at the sound of the divine bell. They plunged themselves into the ocean, never to bother him again. Saint Patrick had been so effective in sending evil away that legend says evil was not found in Ireland for seven years thereafter.

Despite this act, the saint could not come down yet from his mount. He had rid the nation of its demons, but now he had to contend with God himself. Much like the biblical story of Jacob, Patrick had to secure the spiritual interest of his flock. His guardian angel had brought him an announcement that stated he was to be rewarded for his devotion to prayer and penance. He was advised that as many of his people as possible would find themselves in heaven. There would be people stretching as far as the eye could see—from the corners of the land to the sea, all would be welcomed into heaven. Patrick continued his practices of fasting and prayer until he could be sure that the promises made in the announcement brought to him came to fruition. His angel continued to come to him and tell Patrick that he could be certain of his peoples' salvation. But Patrick did not let up in his exercises; he would not go lax in his penance. He waited and prayed, repented and fasted until he could be sure all would be done.

Finally, the message that Patrick sought came to him; his prayers had been heard. Patrick received the good news that many souls would not have to endure purgatory due to his intercession. Patrick also learned that whoever chose to recite his hymn in the spirit of penance before their death would attain the ultimate reward of Heaven, which is eternal life. Patrick also learned that barbarian tribes would not influence his church or otherwise obtain sway. The saint also learned that seven years before Judgement Day, the sea would rise and spread itself all over Ireland as a means of saving the people from temptation and the terrible acts of the Antichrist. Most importantly, Patrick learned of the holiest duty he would undertake yet. Patrick was told that he would judge the entire Irish race on the last day.

The legend goes that Patrick's hard work was rewarded in the most divine of ways. His constant prayer, penance, fasting, and speaking with God, coupled with his true love and devotion of all things heavenly, brought salvation to the people of Ireland.

Chapter Nine

The Death of Saint Patrick

"I pray to God to give me perseverance and to design that I be a faithful witness to Him to the end of my life for my God."

—Saint Patrick

Patrick had now completed what he was set out to do. He had successfully driven out the pagans and their religion from Ireland. He had gathered the Irish people into the beliefs of Christ. Thus, he was ready to prepare for the summons and take his reward.

Saint Brigid, a well-renowned nun, came to Patrick with her chosen fellow nuns. She brought the shroud in which Patrick would be enshrined. The legend goes that Patrick and Saint Brigid began their last prayer, and it was then that a divine vision was shown to the saint. The vision showed all of Ireland lit up with the rays of divine faith. The brightness continued for centuries. But suddenly, the vision turned. Cloud cover appeared and blanketed the island, surrounding it. The religious glory once shown was now fading away. It continued to fade over many centuries until it would show only in remote valleys—and even then, it was just a small fleck of light here and there. Saint Patrick prayed that the light would never be extinguished. It was then that the angel who had spoken to him previously appeared and assured him that this apostolate would never fade out of existence. Patrick continued to pray, and the light began to reappear. It grew in its brightness. It did not stop until all the hills, valleys, and corners of Ireland were awash in the joyous, divine light. The angel then announced to Patrick that this would be the way the nation would look from now on.

Now that his journey was complete, Patrick received the summon to claim his reward on March 17, 493 CE. His last sacraments were administered by Saint Tassach. His remains were to be placed within a shroud woven by the hands of Saint Brigid. Bishops, clergy, and all people of the faith from across the country came to pay respects to their beloved Patrick. On the night of Patrick's passing, the plain's air was filled with the sounds of devoted followers chanting psalms. The darkness was banished by the light of many torches the devotees held in honor of the saint.

It is reported that for several days after Patrick's passing, the light of heaven shone brightly around his bier. The remains of Patrick were said to be interred upon consecrated ground at the local chieftain's fort, two miles from Saul, the site of Patrick's first church.

Conclusion

Saint Patrick is purported to be buried at the Down Cathedral located in County Down, next to Saint Brigid and Saint Columba. Patrick's legacy lives on centuries after his death. The influence of this saint has been far-reaching. Even after his death, saints in the forthcoming years yearned to know and learn from this man. Countless churches and cathedrals were dedicated in Patrick's name. Collum Cille, a missionary, removed three relics from Patrick's tomb, one of which was the bell used by Saint Patrick, his goblet, and the Angel's Gospel. The relics were not removed for personal gain, but rather to remind Ireland of their hero and keep the saint at the forefront of the nation's mind. There even exists a tooth that Patrick supposedly lost while traversing the Sligo coast in search of more converts. It is kept in the National Museum of Ireland for all to see.

In his adopted home of Ireland, Patrick's namesake can be found on several landmarks and areas. Some notable places in Ireland include Ardpatrick of County Limerick, which means "high place of Patrick," or St. Patrick's Island, located in Dublin. Several relics belonging to the saint remain on display for pilgrims and historians alike to view and learn from. For example, the Bell of Saint Patrick is available at the National Museum of Ireland as well as the shrine that encases the instrument. Even in other nations, Patrick remains a positive influence. In Puerto Rico, for example, the city of

Loiza is home to a church bearing the name of Saint Patrick, representative of the faith of many Irish immigrants who settled there during the eighteenth century.

Perhaps the way the modern world most remembers the legacy and good works of the patron saint of Ireland is the Saint Patrick's Day celebrations that take place across the Christian world on March 17 every year. Saint Patrick is fondly remembered across the world on the day of his passing. It is on this day that modern Christians celebrate Patrick's life and contributions to their faith. This day was made into a feast day as early as the seventeenth century and is observed by several churches including those of the Anglican, Catholic, Lutheran, and Eastern Orthodox faiths.

Saint Patrick's Day is a celebration of Saint Patrick and his arrival in Ireland, which brought the ultimate gift to the people. It is a day to celebrate the legacy of the saint, Irish history and culture, and to celebrate Christianity. Celebrations involve parades and festivals. Dancers trained in the art of Irish stepdance perform their craft. Traditional Irish music is played. Citizens wear green clothing and carry shamrocks as a nod to Patrick's teaching of the Holy Trinity. Traditions are upheld, such as floating the shamrock. In this custom, a shamrock is placed into the bottom of a cup of cider, whiskey, or beer. The glass is then toasted to Saint Patrick, and the shamrock is swallowed or tossed over the shoulder for good luck. The wearing of green is an important tradition for Saint Patrick's Day revelers. The green reflects the color of the shamrock and is also a color closely associated with Ireland.

The best way to experience Patrick is to read his works and study his relics. *Confessio* and *Epistola* are readily available for perusal as are the relics that he once used. From this, the saint becomes less the stuff of legend and more a concrete, beloved figure many are still revering today.

Made in United States
Orlando, FL
12 March 2024

44667727R00024